Milly, Molly
Mountain

"We may look different
but we feel the same."

Charlie owned a magnificent, striped,
hot air balloon.

Every Sunday he flew up, up, up and over the mountain.

"Please Charlie, can we go too?" asked Milly. "We want to see what is on the other side of the mountain," said Molly.

Charlie offered a helping hand.
"Come on then, in you get," he said.

Milly and Molly looked at Marmalade
and Tom Cat.
"Alright," said Charlie. "They can
come too."

It was magic.

The roofs were bright red.

The river looked long and blue and curly.

The trees were in straight rows.

The grass was so green.
And everything looked very neat and tidy.

They followed the river, climbed over the trees and flew up, up, up the mountain…

and over the top!

But as far as the eye could see there were clouds, clouds and more clouds.

The wind got stronger and stronger
and blew the balloon higher and higher.
"I don't like this," said Charlie.

"I don't like this at all. Hang on very tightly
now and don't let go."

Suddenly it was not so magic.
"Please can we go home now Charlie?"
cried Milly.
"Please Charlie," wailed Molly.

"I'm doing my best," said Charlie.
And down they began to go. Faster and faster.

Molly turned green.

Milly turned white.

Marmalade and Tom Cat's ears lay flat on their heads. And all their tummies turned inside out.

"Hold on very, very tightly now," ordered
Charlie. And with a bump the basket hit
the ground.

Charlie, Milly, Molly, Marmalade and
Tom Cat flipped out in a pile.

"Let's go home now," suggested Milly.
"We like our side of the mountain best,"
said Molly.

"Come on," agreed Charlie.
"There's no place like home."